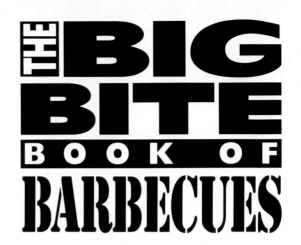

THE BIG BITE
BOOK OF
BARBECUES

THE BIG BITE BOOK OF BARBECUES

MEG JANSZ

a Salamander book
Published by Salamander Books Limited
LONDON

A SALAMANDER BOOK

Published by Salamander Books Ltd,
129-137 York Way
London N7 9LG
United Kingdom

© Salamander Books Ltd, 1995

ISBN 0 86101 789 7

1 2 3 4 5 6 7 8 9 10

All correspondence concerning the content of this volume should be addressed to Salamander Books Ltd.

CREDITS
Author and home economist: Meg Jansz
Home economist's assistant:
    Lucy Pitcairn-Knowles
Managing editor: Lisa Dyer
Photographer: Ken Field
Designer: Ian Sandom
Stylist: Marian Price
Filmset: SX Composing Ltd, England
Colour Separation: P&W Graphics Pte, Ltd,
    Singapore

Printed in Singapore

When making any of the recipes in this book, you should follow either the metric or Imperial measures, as these are not interchangeable.

Other titles of interest:
The Big Bite Book of BURGERS
The Big Bite Book of PIZZAS
The Big Bite Book of SALADS

CONTENTS

INTRODUCTION

The Big Bite Book of Barbecues contains a delicious selection of varied recipes to suit all tastes and occasions. Contrary to the popular belief that barbecues cater primarily for the meat-eater, barbecuing is evolving fast to suit all contemporary tastes. The recipes in the book demonstrate the versatility of barbecuing, with an entire chapter devoted to imaginative vegetable-based barbecues.

Historically, barbecuing was the original style of cooking, with our ancestors of centuries ago spit-roasting whole animals over live coals. In more recent times, the art of barbecuing has evolved to become, in modern societies, a popular way of eating 'al fresco'.

CHARCOAL OR WOOD BARBECUES

Whether they are permanent features, made from a brick base, or portable, most barbecues are designed for just grilling food. They consist of a firebox that holds the fuel and an adjustable rack, which enables you to place food at different heights above the fuel.

There are two types of coal fuel that can be used: lumpwood charcoal is cheaper, easier to light and burns hotter than its alternative, pressed briquettes. However, once briquettes have been lit they last a lot longer.

Fire lighters or lighting ignition fluid are also essential to start the barbecue. Fire lighters should be placed in the bottom of the firebox, and a 7.5-cm (3-inch) pyramid of charcoal constructed over the top. The fire lighters are then ignited with a taper to start the fire. Use ignition fluid to help the fire, if necessary.

Once the barbecue is lit, it can take up to one hour to reach the 'ashen coal or wood

stage', which means the barbecue is ready to cook on. Please remember to follow the manufacturer's instructions carefully if you are using ignition fluid. Ensure the hot coals are spread out evenly. To maintain the heat, gradually add fresh coal around the outer edges.

Wood can also be used as a fuel, but is more difficult to start. If you use wood, use hardwoods which burn longer. Allow the flames to die right down before cooking. Wood barbecues will take 30-45 minutes to reach the point where they are ready for cooking.

Aromatic wood chips are available for use on barbecues to impart flavours to the food. Oak and hickory wood chips are especially popular and there are also more unusual ones, like mesquite and cherry. Wood chips should be soaked for about 30 minutes in cold water, then drained and placed on the ashen coals.

GAS BARBECUES

These barbecues only need 5 or 10 minutes to heat and the temperature can be easily controlled. Gas barbecues either have vaporizer bars or lava rocks that are heated up by gas burners. The cooking rack is set above these. Moisture drips from the cooking food on to the bars and vaporizes to give the food an aromatic smoked flavour. Pre-soaked wood chips can also be placed in a foil container on the vaporizer bar, or on the heated lava rocks, but do not put food too near the container.

RIGHT: Fish, seafood, vegetables, meat and even certain cheeses barbecue well, and you may want to try the Mushroom & Mozzarella Brochettes (see page 64), pictured here.

GENERAL SAFETY

Always place the barbecue on even ground and away from trees, buildings or fences. Once the barbecue is alight, do not leave it un-attended, and keep children away from it.

Allow embers to cool completely before disposing. They will take several hours to cool. Allow transportable barbecues to cool com-pletely before packing them away. Always use long-handled tongs when handling food on the barbecue. Never use petrol or similar flamm-able liquids to light a barbecue and keep matches well away from the barbecue. Have a bottle of water handy to douse the flames if they become too unruly.

FOOD SAFETY AND COOKING

Keep raw food out of the sun. Make sure that pieces of meat and sausages are well cooked. Adequate lighting around a barbecue is essen-tial at night to check whether food is properly cooked. Never cook frozen food on a barbe-cue – it must always be thoroughly defrosted.

All the recipes should be cooked over a medium-hot barbecue, unless otherwise in-dicated. Barbecuing is a rather unpredictable cooking method, and you will need to adjust the cooking times according to the intensity of your barbecue. If you find the barbecue is becoming too hot, simply raise the grill to the next setting on your barbecue.

EQUIPMENT

There is a large array of barbecue equipment for sale these days, but there are a few essen-tial pieces. Wear an apron to prevent splatters on clothes and use well-padded oven gloves to handle hot metal skewers and griddle plates. Long-handled tongs, a fork and a fish slice are

essential for turning food. Use metal skewers for more robust food, oiling them first. Wood skewers should be used for delicate foods. Soak them in cold water before use to prevent them catching fire. When barbecuing food in foil parcels, use heavy-duty foil.

A wide range of hinged wire racks are avail-able for barbecuing. These are especially useful for fish and fragile food. Metal griddle plates that can be heated on the barbecue are useful for cooking fragile foods that would otherwise be tricky to cook on a barbecue. Always oil the heated griddle plate before placing food on it. A stiff wire brush is essential for brushing down the grill bars after use and use a metal scraper for removing any burnt food.

MARINADES

Marinating plays a vital part in barbecuing, as it adds extra depth of flavour. Fish and shellfish generally require a shorter marinating time than meat. If food has been marinated in the refrigerator, allow it to come back to room temperature before cooking.

Marinades that contain acidic elements, like vinegar or citrus juice, will tenderize the food. Oils in marinades help prevent food from sticking and herbs and spices create mouth-watering flavours. All in all, marinating can turn the simplest cut of meat or piece of fish or vegetable into something more special.

Barbecuing should be an enjoyable way of cooking, so do not rush. Above all, relax, enjoy this sociable way of cooking and eating, and savour the tantalizing aromas and tastes that barbecuing produces.

RIGHT: Using marinades to brush meat and vegetables while barbecuing adds extra flavour.

QUICK BARBECUES

A range of 'fuss-free' recipes are included in this chapter, all which take a minimum of time to prepare and would be suitable for impromptu summer meals or weekday family meals. Although certain recipes, such as Spare Ribs with Tangy BBQ Sauce and Horseradish Steaks, benefit from being marinated for several hours before cooking, as this provides a better depth of flavour, the end result will still be tasty if you do not have the time to marinate.

TERIYAKI RIBS

1.4 kg (3 lb) meaty pork spare ribs
Salad and crusty bread, to serve (optional)

MARINADE
90 ml (6 tbsp) clear honey
45 ml (3 tbsp) dark soy sauce
90 ml (6 tbsp) tomato ketchup
7.5 ml (1½ tsp) cracked black pepper
10 ml (2 tsp) Chinese five-spice powder
Grated zest and juice of 1 large orange

Mix the marinade ingredients together in a bowl. Place the spare ribs in a large glass dish and pour the marinade over them. Turn the ribs to coat evenly. Cover and refrigerate for 2-3 hours, if time permits.

Remove the ribs from the marinade, reserving the marinade for basting. Cook the ribs on a prepared barbecue for about 20 minutes, basting frequently. Serve with salad and crusty bread, if desired.   SERVES 4-6

SPARE RIBS WITH TANGY BBQ SAUCE

1.4 kg (3 lb) meaty pork spare ribs

TANGY BBQ SAUCE
2 cloves garlic, crushed
90 ml (6 tbsp) clear honey
30 ml (2 tbsp) tomato purée
30 ml (2 tbsp) chilli sauce
30 ml (2 tbsp) Worcestershire sauce
30 ml (2 tbsp) soy sauce
20 ml (4 tsp) American yellow mustard
Juice of 1 lemon

Mix the sauce ingredients together in a bowl. Place the spare ribs in a large glass dish and pour the sauce over the ribs, turning the ribs to coat evenly. Cover and refrigerate for 2 hours, if time permits.

Remove ribs from the barbecue sauce and pour the remaining sauce into a small saucepan. Cook the ribs on a prepared barbecue for about 20 minutes, turning frequently. Just before serving, reheat the sauce. Bring the sauce to the boil and boil rapidly for 2-3 minutes. Serve the ribs hot, passing the sauce separately.

SERVES 4-6

RIGHT: Teriyaki Ribs

HORSERADISH STEAKS WITH BBQ VEGETABLES

4 sirloin steaks, weighing about 150 g (5 oz) each

MARINADE
30 ml (2 tbsp) horseradish sauce
30 ml (2 tbsp) cracked black pepper
60 ml (4 tbsp) vegetable oil
Pinch of salt

HORSERADISH SAUCE
60 ml (4 tbsp) soured cream
15 ml (1 tbsp) horseradish sauce
Salt and ground black pepper

BBQ VEGETABLES
4 medium courgettes, halved lengthways
2 red peppers, cored, seeded and quartered
4 shallots, unpeeled and halved
Salt and ground black pepper
Oil for brushing

Mix the marinade ingredients together in a bowl. Place the steaks in a shallow glass dish and pour over the marinade. Turn the steaks to coat evenly, cover and refrigerate for 2 hours.

Mix the sauce ingredients together in a bowl, cover and refrigerate until required.

Season the vegetables and brush them liberally with oil. Cook them on a prepared barbecue, turning occasionally and basting with oil. The courgettes require about 12 minutes to cook, the peppers 10 minutes, and the shallots 8 minutes. Keep all the vegetables warm while cooking the steaks.

Cook the steaks on the barbecue, brushing them occasionally with the marinade. For a medium-cooked steak, cook for about 3 minutes each side. Decrease or increase the cooking time if a rare or well-done steak is required. Serve the steaks hot with the Horseradish Sauce and the BBQ Vegetables. SERVES 4

COFFEE BEAN & MOLASSES RIBS

1.4 kg (3 lb) pork spare ribs
45 ml (3 tbsp) molasses or treacle
60 ml (4 tbsp) vegetable oil
120 ml (8 tbsp) coarsely ground coffee beans
Salad and jacket potatoes, to serve (optional)

Place the spare ribs in a large glass dish. Mix the molasses, oil and coffee beans together in a bowl and pour over the ribs, turning the ribs to coat evenly. Cover and refrigerate for 2-3 hours, if time permits.

Remove the ribs from the dish, reserving any remaining mixture for basting. Cook the ribs on a prepared barbecue for about 20 minutes, turning and basting them frequently. Serve with salad and jacket potatoes, if desired. SERVES 4-6

TOP: Coffee Bean & Molasses Ribs
BOTTOM: Horseradish Steaks with BBQ Vegetables

LIVER & BACON BROCHETTES WITH GRILLED RED ONION

450 g (1 lb) lamb's liver
16 rashers streaky bacon
8 wooden or metal skewers
60 ml (4 tbsp) chopped fresh sage
90 ml (6 tbsp) olive oil
Sea salt and ground black pepper
4 small red onions, unpeeled and halved
Salad and potatoes, to serve (optional)

Cut the lamb's liver into fairly large chunks. Remove the rind from the bacon rashers and roll up each rasher. Thread the liver chunks and two bacon rolls on to each skewer.

Mix together the sage and oil, season, and brush the oil all over the prepared brochettes and the halved onions. Cook the onions on a prepared barbecue for about 8 minutes on each side, brushing occasionally with the sage oil.

Cook the liver and bacon brochettes on the barbecue for 4-5 minutes on each side, brushing frequently with the sage oil. Serve at once with salad and potatoes, if desired. SERVES 4

LAMB CHOPS WITH GARLIC, LEMON & OREGANO

4 cloves garlic
20 ml (4 tsp) chopped fresh oregano
Grated zest and juice of 2 small lemons
60 ml (4 tbsp) sunflower oil
Sea salt and ground black pepper
8 lamb chops

Preheat an oven grill to hot. Place the garlic cloves under the grill for 8-10 minutes, turning them occasionally, until the skins are charred and the garlic cloves feel soft. Squeeze the roasted garlic out of its skin into a bowl, and mash to a paste. Add the oregano, lemon zest and juice, oil and seasoning. Mix well to combine thoroughly.

Place the lamb chops in a shallow bowl and pour over the roasted garlic mixture. Cover and refrigerate for 2 hours, if time permits.

Remove the chops from the garlic mixture, reserving the remaining mixture. Cook the chops on a prepared barbecue for about 5 minutes on each side. Just before serving, heat up the reserved garlic mixture in a small saucepan and pour it over the barbecued chops. Serve at once. SERVES 4

RIGHT: Liver & Bacon Brochettes with Grilled Red Onion

BEEF & BEAN BURGERS

450 g (1 lb) minced beef
225 g (8 oz) canned red kidney beans, drained
and chopped
1 small onion, finely chopped
2 cloves garlic, crushed
5 ml (1 tsp) chilli powder
Salt and ground black pepper
A little oil for brushing
50 g (2 oz) crisp green lettuce leaves
4 thick slices avocado
1 red onion, sliced into rings
60 ml (4 tbsp) coriander leaves
4 flour tortillas, warmed
60 ml (4 tbsp) soured cream
Pickled Mexican chillies, to serve

Place the beef, beans, onion, garlic, chilli powder and salt and pepper in a bowl and mix well to combine. Divide the mixture into four and shape into equal-sized patties. Chill until required.

Just before cooking, brush each burger with a little oil. Cook on a prepared barbecue for about 6 minutes on each side for a medium-cooked burger. Decrease or increase the cooking time for either a rare or well-done burger.

Divide the lettuce, avocado, sliced onion and coriander between the tortillas. Top each with a burger and spoon some soured cream on each one. Serve the burgers with pickled chillies.   SERVES 4

CALIFORNIA DOGS

4 large frankfurters
4 plain or granary hot dog rolls, split lengthways
A little softened butter
6 Cos lettuce leaves, torn into bite-sized pieces
4 small tomatoes, sliced
1 small onion, sliced into rings

SWEETCORN SALSA

198-g (7-oz) can sweetcorn kernels, drained
¼ green pepper, finely diced
4 radishes, thinly sliced
½ red onion, finely diced
1 clove garlic, crushed
Juice of ½ lemon
15 ml (1 tbsp) chopped fresh parsley
Salt and ground black pepper

Place the ingredients for the salsa in a bowl and mix together gently to combine. Cover and refrigerate.

Make several diagonal slashes in each frankfurter and cook them on a prepared barbecue for 4 minutes on each side. Place the hot dog rolls, cut-side down, on the barbecue to toast them lightly. Spread a little softened butter on the rolls.

Divide the lettuce, tomato and onion between the four rolls and top each with a frankfurter. Serve them at once with the Sweetcorn Salsa.   SERVES 4

TOP: California Dog
BOTTOM: Beef & Bean Burger

MEDITERRANEAN CHARGRILLED SARDINES

The sardines in this recipe are cooked on pairs of skewers, but you could also use a metal fish rack that holds 6 or 12 sardines.

12 sardines
12 small lemon zest strips
12 small rosemary sprigs
8 long bamboo skewers, soaked in cold water
for 2 hours
4 lemon wedges

HERB AND LEMON OIL
60 ml (4 tbsp) extra virgin olive oil
10 ml (2 tsp) grated lemon zest
Juice of 1 lemon
15 ml (1 tbsp) chopped fresh rosemary
15 ml (1 tbsp) chopped fresh thyme
Salt and ground black pepper

Using a pair of small scissors, slit the bellies of the sardines and discard the guts. Wash the sardines and dry them on kitchen paper. Stuff a small strip of lemon zest and a rosemary sprig into the cavity of each sardine.

Thread three sardines on to each pair of skewers by pushing one skewer through a sardine just below the head and pushing the second skewer in just above the tail. Thread on the other two sardines in the same way, then repeat the process with the remaining sardines and skewers.

Mix the ingredients for the herb oil together, and brush liberally over the sardines. Cook the sardines on a prepared, very hot barbecue for 3-4 minutes on each side, basting with more oil while they are cooking.

Slide the cooked sardines off the skewers and serve at once with lemon wedges.　　　SERVES 4

SALMON WITH CAPERS & GAZPACHO SALSA

4 salmon steaks, weighing about 100 g (4 oz) each

MARINADE
45 ml (3 tbsp) olive oil
Zest and juice of 1 lime
15 ml (1 tbsp) capers in brine, drained
Pinch of sea salt

GAZPACHO SALSA
4 small tomatoes, peeled, seeded and diced
150 g (5 oz) cucumber, diced
½ onion, diced
½ red pepper, diced
15 ml (1 tbsp) chopped fresh parsley
20 ml (4 tsp) chopped fresh coriander
5 ml (1 tsp) caster sugar
30 ml (2 tbsp) red wine vinegar
Salt and ground black pepper

Mix the marinade ingredients together in a bowl. Place the salmon steaks in a shallow dish and pour over the marinade. Cover and refrigerate the salmon for 2 hours, if time permits.

Place the ingredients for the salsa in a bowl and mix together gently to combine. Cover and refrigerate until required.

Remove the salmon steaks from the marinade and press a few capers into the flesh of each piece of salmon. Reserve the remaining marinade for basting. Cook the salmon on a prepared barbecue for 4-5 minutes on each side, turning the fish once and basting occasionally. Serve the salmon hot with the salsa.

SERVES 4

TOP: Mediterranean Chargrilled Sardines
BOTTOM: Salmon with Capers &
Gazpacho Salsa

GRILLED TUNA WITH TOMATO & OLIVE SALSA

4 tuna steaks, weighing about 150 g (5 oz) each

OLIVE MARINADE
60 ml (4 tbsp) green olive purée
120 ml (8 tbsp) olive oil
3 cloves garlic, crushed
Salt and ground black pepper

TOMATO AND OLIVE SALSA
15 black olives, stoned and sliced
4 tomatoes, peeled, seeded and sliced
75 g (3 oz) sun-dried tomatoes in oil,
drained and sliced
4 spring onions, sliced
14 basil leaves, torn
Pinch of sugar

Mix the marinade ingredients together in a large shallow dish. Add the tuna steaks, turning to coat evenly. Cover and refrigerate for 2 hours, if time permits.

Make the salsa by combining all the ingredients together. Refrigerate until required.

Remove the tuna steaks from the marinade, reserving the marinade for basting. Cook the steaks on a prepared barbecue for about 5 minutes on each side, basting occasionally. Serve the grilled tuna at once with the salsa.　　　　　SERVES 4

MESQUITE-SMOKED FISH

Use a solid-fleshed fish for this recipe, such as catfish or monkfish.

4 pieces catfish or monkfish tail with the bone,
weighing about 200 g (7 oz) each
About 1 cup mesquite chips, soaked in cold water
for 1 hour
Skewered New Potatoes, to serve (see page 74)

MARINADE
120 ml (8 tbsp) extra virgin olive oil
60 ml (4 tbsp) white wine vinegar
4 cloves garlic, crushed
10 ml (2 tsp) tropical peppercorns, crushed
10 ml (2 tsp) chopped fennel fronds (optional)
A little sea salt

Mix the marinade ingredients together in a bowl. Place the fish portions in a shallow dish and pour over the marinade, turning the fish to coat evenly. Cover and refrigerate for 2 hours, if time permits.

Drain the soaked mesquite chips and scatter them over the hot coals of a prepared barbecue. Remove the fish from the marinade, reserving the marinade for basting. Cook the fish on the barbecue for about 15 minutes, or until cooked through, turning and basting occasionally. Serve at once with some Skewered New Potatoes, if desired.　　　　　SERVES 4

RIGHT: Grilled Tuna with Tomato & Olive Salsa

TIGER PRAWNS WITH CORIANDER MAYONNAISE

16 raw tiger prawns in their shells, with
heads removed
4 wooden or metal skewers

MARINADE
120 ml (8 tbsp) sweet chilli sauce
60 ml (4 tbsp) tomato purée
20 ml (4 tsp) lemon juice
4 cloves garlic, crushed
20 ml (4 tsp) sesame oil

CORIANDER MAYONNAISE
90 ml (6 tbsp) mayonnaise
½ fresh red chilli, seeded and finely chopped
½ small red onion, finely chopped
30 ml (2 tbsp) chopped fresh coriander
30 ml (2 tbsp) lemon juice
Salt and ground black pepper

Mix the marinade ingredients together in a bowl. Add the prawns to the marinade and toss to coat evenly. Cover and refrigerate for 2 hours, if time permits.

Mix the mayonnaise ingredients together, cover and refrigerate until required.

Thread four prawns on to each skewer and cook them on a prepared barbecue for 4-5 minutes on each side, turning them once. To serve, remove prawns from skewers, if preferred, and serve with the Coriander Mayonnaise. SERVES 2

CHARGRILLED LOBSTER WITH HERB BUTTER

Ask your fishmonger to split the lobsters in half, ready for the barbecue. Otherwise, kill each lobster by piercing with a knife at the central point where the head meets the body. Halve the head and split in half along the body.

2 raw lobsters, each weighing about 450 g (1 lb),
split in half lengthways with claws cracked
Salt and ground black pepper

HERB BUTTER
40 g (1½ oz) butter, softened
15 ml (1 tbsp) chopped fresh chervil
5 ml (1 tsp) snipped fresh chives
5 ml (1 tsp) finely chopped shallot
Squeeze of lemon juice
Salt and ground black pepper

Place the ingredients for the Herb Butter in a bowl and beat together to combine. Place the flavoured butter in a sausage shape on a piece of greaseproof paper or cling film. Roll up the butter to produce a cylinder and refrigerate to harden the butter.

Season the lobster flesh lightly with salt and pepper and cook the lobster halves, cut-side down, on a prepared barbecue for 8-10 minutes, until the flesh has become opaque and the shells have turned orange.

Cook the claws separately. They are cooked when the shells have turned bright orange. Serve the freshly grilled lobster with discs of Herb Butter. SERVES 2

TOP: Chargrilled Lobster with Herb Butter
BOTTOM: Tiger Prawns with
Coriander Mayonnaise

SPICY & EXOTIC BARBECUES

Influenced by the cuisines of Mexico, the Mediterranean and the Far East, the recipes in this chapter are robustly flavoured. Chillies, coriander, ginger, lime and sesame are ingredients that feature predominantly in the recipes. An exciting selection of chicken, meat, fish and seafood dishes are included, from the spicy Turmeric Prawn & Pineapple Skewers to the unusual Halibut Chargrilled in Banana Leaves.

MUSTARD-GLAZED CHICKEN DRUMSTICKS

8 chicken drumsticks

MUSTARD MARINADE
30 ml (2 tbsp) clear honey
10 ml (2 tsp) English mustard
10 ml (2 tsp) coarse-grain mustard
10 ml (2 tsp) Worcestershire sauce
Juice of 1 orange
2 cloves garlic, crushed
½ onion, very finely chopped

Make several deep slashes through the skin of each drumstick and place the chicken in a shallow glass dish.

Mix the marinade ingredients together and pour over the drumsticks. Turn the drumsticks so they are evenly coated in marinade. Cover and refrigerate for 2-3 hours or overnight.

Remove the drumsticks from the marinade, re-serving the marinade for basting, and cook the chicken on a prepared barbecue for about 20 minutes, turning occasionally and basting during cooking. To test that the chicken is cooked, pierce the flesh with a skewer. If the juices run clear, the chicken is ready to serve.

SERVES 4

BARBECUED CHICKEN WITH CHILLI & LIME

6 boneless chicken breasts

MARINADE
20 ml (4 tsp) chilli oil
30 ml (2 tbsp) clear honey
60 ml (4 tbsp) chopped fresh coriander
2 cloves garlic, crushed
Grated zest and juice of 2 limes

CORIANDER AND CHILLI YOGHURT
120 ml (8 tbsp) Greek yoghurt
2.5 ml (½ tsp) chilli oil
Grated zest and juice of 1 lime
60 ml (4 tbsp) chopped fresh coriander
1 small fresh red chilli, seeded and finely chopped
A little salt

Place the marinade ingredients in a shallow glass dish and mix well to combine. With a sharp knife, make several deep slashes in each chicken and place the chicken breasts in the marinade, turning to coat well. Cover and refrigerate for 3-4 hours.

Mix the yoghurt ingredients together in a bowl. Cover and refrigerate until required.

Remove the chicken from the marinade, reserving the marinade for basting. Place the chicken, skin-side up, on a prepared, medium-hot barbecue. Cook the chicken breasts for 10 minutes, brushing occasionally with the marinade, then turn over and cook for a further 10 minutes. To test if the chicken is cooked, pierce the thickest part of the breast with a skewer. If the juices are still pink, cook until the juices run clear. Serve at once with the yoghurt.

SERVES 6

RIGHT: Barbecued Chicken with Chilli & Lime

MEXICAN FISH KEBABS

550 g (1¼ lb) red snapper fillets, cut into chunks
4 mini red peppers, halved, or 8 pickled
cherry peppers
2 onions, cut into 8 wedges each
8 wooden or metal skewers
Spicy Rice, to serve (see page 72)

MARINADE
60 ml (4 tbsp) chopped fresh coriander
60 ml (4 tbsp) olive oil
Juice of 3 limes
20 ml (4 tsp) paprika
I fresh red chilli, seeded and finely chopped

GUACAMOLE
2 avocados
Juice of I large lime
½ onion, finely chopped
90 ml (6 tbsp) torn coriander leaves
Salt and ground black pepper

Place the marinade ingredients in a shallow glass bowl and mix well to combine. Add the chunks of fish and turn to coat evenly. Cover and refrigerate for 2 hours.

Make the Guacamole. Mash the avocados with the lime juice. Stir in the other ingredients, taste and adjust seasoning, and refrigerate until required.

Thread the marinated fish on to the skewers, alternating with the peppers and onion wedges. Reserve the marinade for basting. Cook the kebabs on a prepared barbecue for about 10 minutes, turning and brushing them with the reserved marinade. Serve at once with the Guacamole and Spicy Rice.   SERVES 4

HALIBUT CHARGRILLED IN BANANA LEAVES

Galangal is used in this recipe for its exotic taste, but you can substitute fresh root ginger. Heavy-duty foil can also be substituted for the banana leaves, but the foil will not need to be oiled.

450-g (1-lb) piece skinless, boneless halibut, cut into
2.5-cm (1-inch) cubes
4 pieces banana leaf, about 31 cm (12 inches) square
Oil for brushing
Cocktail sticks

SPICY PASTE
I large dried red chilli
5-cm (2-inch) piece galangal, peeled and chopped
2 stalks lemon grass, finely chopped
2 cloves garlic, crushed
I shallot, finely chopped
2 Kaffir lime leaves, finely chopped
15 ml (1 tbsp) Thai fish sauce
45 ml (3 tbsp) groundnut oil

Prepare the Spicy Paste. Soak the red chilli in hot water for 10 minutes, then drain and chop finely. Place the chilli and the remaining ingredients in a spice grinder or food processor and blend to a smooth paste.

Transfer the paste to a shallow glass dish, add the cubed fish and toss the fish to coat evenly. Cover and refrigerate for 2 hours.

Brush the banana leaves with a little oil and divide the marinated fish between them. Wrap up to form parcels and secure with cocktail sticks. Brush the outside of the parcels with a little oil and cook the fish parcels on a prepared barbecue for about 10 minutes, until the fish is cooked through.   SERVES 4

TOP: Halibut Chargrilled in Banana Leaves
BOTTOM: Mexican Fish Kebabs

SCALLOP BROCHETTES WITH GINGER & ORANGE

16 large scallops
4 long strips of orange zest
350 g (12 oz) courgettes, canelled and cut into 12 chunks
4 metal skewers

MARINADE
Juice of 2 oranges
20 ml (4 tsp) grated fresh root ginger
60 ml (4 tbsp) vegetable oil
4 spring onions, finely chopped
2 cloves garlic, crushed
Salt and ground black pepper

GINGER AND ORANGE BUTTER
100 g (4 oz) butter, softened
15 ml (1 tbsp) grated fresh root ginger
15 ml (1 tbsp) grated orange zest
15 ml (1 tbsp) orange juice
Salt and ground black pepper

Mix the marinade ingredients together in a large, shallow bowl. Add the scallops to the marinade and turn to coat evenly. Cover and refrigerate for 2 hours.

Mix the ingredients for the butter together and place the butter in a sausage shape on a piece of greaseproof paper or cling film. Roll up to form a cylinder and refrigerate until the butter hardens.

Remove the scallops from the marinade, reserving the marinade for basting. Thread four scallops, a strip of orange zest and three chunks of courgette on to each skewer. Cook the brochettes on a prepared, medium-hot barbecue for 8-10 minutes, turning and brushing them frequently with the marinade. Serve the hot brochettes with discs of flavoured butter, so the butter melts over the scallops and courgettes.

SERVES 4

TURMERIC PRAWN & PINEAPPLE SKEWERS

24 raw tiger prawns, peeled but with tails intact
8 wooden or metal skewers
225 g (8 oz) fresh pineapple, cut into 16 chunks
16 bulbous white parts of spring onion

TURMERIC MARINADE
1 stalk lemon grass, finely chopped
2.5-cm (1-inch) piece fresh root ginger, peeled and grated
2 cloves garlic, crushed
30 ml (2 tbsp) groundnut oil
15 ml (1 tbsp) lemon juice
5 ml (1 tsp) turmeric
Pinch of sugar
Salt and ground black pepper

Place the marinade ingredients in a food processor and blend to a paste. Transfer the paste to a large bowl, add the prawns and turn to coat evenly. Refrigerate for 2-3 hours or overnight.

Thread the marinated prawns on to the skewers, alternating with the pineapple chunks and spring onions. Reserve the marinade for basting. Cook the prawn skewers on a prepared barbecue for 8-10 minutes, turning and basting them while they cook. Serve at once.

SERVES 4

LEFT: Turmeric Prawn & Pineapple Skewers
RIGHT: Scallop Brochettes with Ginger & Orange

MALAYSIAN FISH WITH SPICY PEANUT SAUCE

6 medium mackerel, weighing about 200 g (7 oz) each, gutted and cleaned
A wire frame for cooking the fish

MARINADE
60 ml (4 tbsp) sambal oelek (hot pepper condiment)
60 ml (4 tbsp) groundnut oil
10 ml (2 tsp) soft brown sugar
2 cloves garlic, crushed
Juice of 2 limes

SPICY PEANUT SAUCE
15 ml (1 tbsp) tamarind concentrate, mixed with
120 ml (8 tbsp) water
20 ml (4 tsp) soft brown sugar
2 spring onions, chopped
1 stalk lemon grass, chopped
1 clove garlic, crushed
15 ml (1 tbsp) sambal oelek (hot pepper condiment)
75 g (3 oz) salted peanuts, coarsely ground
150 ml (¼ pint) coconut milk

Mix the marinade ingredients together in a bowl. Make several deep slashes in the flesh of each mackerel and place the fish in a large, shallow dish. Pour over the marinade and turn the fish around, coating well. Cover and refrigerate for at least 2 hours.

Make the peanut sauce. Place the first six ingredients in a saucepan, bring to the boil, then reduce the heat and simmer for 5 minutes. Add the peanuts and cook for a further minute, then stir in the coconut milk and simmer for a further 3 minutes. Set aside.

Remove the mackerel from the marinade, reserving the marinade for basting. Cook the fish in a wire frame on a prepared barbecue for about 15 minutes, turning and basting as they cook. Serve the fish with the warm Spicy Peanut Sauce.　　　SERVES 6

PHUKET CRAB CAKES

25 g (1 oz) butter
25 g (1 oz) flour
150 ml (¼ pint) milk
450 g (1 lb) fresh or canned crabmeat, drained and flaked
175 g (6 oz) fresh white breadcrumbs
60 ml (4 tbsp) chopped fresh coriander
30 ml (2 tbsp) grated lime zest
45 ml (3 tbsp) freshly squeezed lime juice
45 ml (3 tbsp) grated fresh root ginger
20 ml (4 tsp) soy sauce
1 fresh red chilli, seeded and finely chopped
Salt and ground black pepper
60 ml (4 tbsp) vegetable oil for brushing
A barbecue griddle plate for cooking
Salad and hot chilli sauce, to serve (optional)

Melt the butter in a saucepan and stir in the flour to make a roux. Gradually add the milk, whisking well between each addition, and boil for 2-3 minutes to form a thick white sauce.

Remove the sauce from the heat and stir in the crab, breadcrumbs, coriander, lime zest and juice, ginger, soy sauce, chilli and seasoning. Leave to cool.

When the mixture is cool, shape it into eight cakes. Refrigerate the crab cakes for at least 2 hours before cooking them.

Oil the griddle and heat it on a prepared barbecue. Brush the crab cakes with some oil and cook on the griddle for 4-5 minutes. Brush with more oil, turn them over and cook for a further 4-5 minutes. Serve at once with a salad and chilli sauce, if desired.　　　SERVES 4

RIGHT: Malaysian Fish with Spicy Peanut Sauce

PORK BROCHETTES WITH CITRUS SALSA

450 g (1 lb) pork tenderloin, cut into 4-cm
(1½-inch) cubes
8 wooden or metal skewers
2 small yellow peppers, cored, seeded and chopped
8 small onions, halved
16 bay leaves

MARINADE

60 ml (4 tbsp) dry sherry or rice wine
60 ml (4 tbsp) ground coriander
60 ml (4 tbsp) sunflower oil
4 cloves garlic, finely chopped
6 Kaffir lime leaves, finely chopped
Salt and ground black pepper

CITRUS SALSA

2 oranges
2 pink grapefruit
10 ml (2 tsp) chopped fresh thyme
20 ml (4 tsp) snipped fresh chives
4 Kaffir lime leaves, very finely chopped
Salt and ground black pepper

Mix the marinade ingredients together in a glass bowl.
Add the cubed pork and mix to coat evenly. Cover and
refrigerate for 4 hours.

Thread the marinated pork on to the skewers,
alternating with the peppers, onions and bay leaves.
Reserve the marinade for basting.

For the salsa, peel the oranges and grapefruit and
cut in between the membranes to produce segments.
Chop the segments roughly. Place in a bowl with the
remaining ingredients and toss gently to combine.

Cook the brochettes over a prepared medium-hot
barbecue for about 15 minutes, turning frequently and
brushing them with the marinade. Serve hot, accom-
panied by the Citrus Salsa.   SERVES 4

THAI-STYLE SKEWERED CHICKEN

4 skinless, boneless chicken breasts, weighing
150 g (5 oz) each
8 wooden or metal skewers
Lime wedges, to serve
Jasmine and Sesame Rice, to serve (see page 72)

THAI MARINADE

30 ml (2 tbsp) Thai red curry paste
30 ml (2 tbsp) ground coriander
45 ml (3 tbsp) groundnut oil
10 ml (2 tsp) ground cumin
10 ml (2 tsp) caster sugar
2 stalks lemon grass, very finely chopped
Juice of 2 limes

Mix the marinade ingredients together in a large bowl.
Cut the chicken into 2.5-cm (1-inch) cubes and add
to the marinade. Turn to coat evenly, cover and refrigerate for 2-3 hours or overnight.

Thread the marinated chicken on to the skewers
and reserve the marinade for basting. Cook the
chicken on a prepared, medium-hot barbecue for
about 7 minutes on each side, basting with the reserved marinade while cooking. Serve with lime
wedges and Jasmine and Sesame Rice, if desired.
SERVES 4

TOP: Thai-style Skewered Chicken
BOTTOM: Pork Brochettes with Citrus Salsa

CHARGRILLED SQUID WITH SESAME & CASHEW

30 ml (2 tbsp) cornflour, sifted
2 egg whites, beaten
10 ml (2 tsp) light soy sauce
5 ml (1 tsp) sesame oil
175 g (6 oz) raw cashew nuts, finely chopped
60 ml (4 tbsp) sesame seeds
12 prepared baby squid tubes
Cocktail sticks
A barbecue griddle plate for cooking
Thai sweet chilli sauce, to serve
Julienne of spring onion and cucumber, to serve

STUFFING

350 g (12 oz) cooked white rice
4 spring onions, finely chopped
10 ml (2 tsp) finely chopped fresh root ginger
5 ml (1 tsp) finely chopped fresh red chilli
10 ml (2 tsp) light soy sauce

Place the stuffing ingredients in a food processor and blend briefly until well combined. Stuff the cavities of the squid with the mixture.

Mix the cornflour, egg whites, soy sauce and sesame oil together. Mix the cashew nuts and sesame seeds together and spread them out on a plate. Dip each stuffed squid tube in the egg mixture and then roll in the cashew nut mixture to coat evenly. Secure the end of each squid tube with a cocktail stick to hold in the stuffing. Chill the coated squid tubes in the refrigerator for 2 hours.

Oil the griddle plate and heat it on a prepared barbecue. Cook the squid on the griddle for about 8 minutes, turning occasionally until golden. Serve hot with chilli sauce and vegetable julienne.   SERVES 4

CHINESE-STYLE SPARE RIBS

1.4 kg (3 lb) meaty pork spare ribs

SZECHUAN MARINADE

4 stalks lemon grass, very finely chopped
60 ml (4 tbsp) Szechuan peppercorns, crushed
60 ml (4 tbsp) dried chilli flakes
60 ml (4 tbsp) groundnut oil
45 ml (3 tbsp) soft brown sugar
20 ml (4 tsp) ground coriander
20 ml (4 tsp) sesame oil

Place the marinade ingredients in a food processor or spice grinder and blend to a paste. Transfer the marinade to a large bowl.

Cut the spare ribes into 10-cm (4-inch) lengths and add to the bowl of marinade. Turn to coat evenly, cover and refrigerate for 2-3 hours or overnight.

Remove the ribs from the marinade, reserving the marinade for basting. Cook the ribs on a prepared barbecue for 15-20 minutes, turning and basting them occasionally. Serve at once.   SERVES 4-6

RIGHT: Chargrilled Squid with Sesame & Cashew

LAMB & APRICOT SKEWERS

550 g (1¼ lb) lamb fillet, cut into 24 pieces
4 shallots
4 firm, ripe apricots, halved
16 bay leaves
8 wooden or metal skewers
Barbecued Artichokes, to serve (optional)

MARINADE
45 ml (3 tbsp) apricot jam
30 ml (2 tbsp) soy sauce
60 ml (4 tbsp) vegetable oil
30 ml (2 tbsp) cider vinegar
3 ml (¾ tsp) cayenne
2 large cloves garlic, crushed
Ground black pepper

Mix the marinade ingredients together in a shallow glass dish. Add the lamb pieces, toss to coat evenly, cover and refrigerate for 2 hours.

Blanch the shallots in boiling water for 4 minutes, then remove and peel and halve them.

Remove the lamb from the marinade, reserving the marinade for basting. Thread three chunks of meat, a shallot half, an apricot half and two bay leaves on to each skewer. Cook the lamb skewers on a prepared barbecue for about 15 minutes, turning and basting them while cooking. Serve hot with Barbecued Artichokes, if desired. SERVES 4

BARBECUED ARTICHOKES

4 small globe artichokes
60 ml (4 tbsp) olive oil
Juice of ½ lemon
Salt and ground black pepper

Trim the artichoke stalks close to the base and cook them in boiling, salted water for 20-25 minutes.

Halve the artichokes and scoop out the hairy chokes. Mix together the oil, lemon juice and seasoning. Brush the artichokes all over with the oil mixture and cook on a prepared barbecue for 10-15 minutes, turning occasionally, until they are lightly charred. Serve hot. SERVES 4

SPICY BEEF KEBABS

550 g (1¼ lb) fillet or rump steak, cut into
bite-sized cubes
1 red pepper
1 green pepper
1 yellow pepper
16 cherry tomatoes
8 metal skewers

GINGER MARINADE
30 ml (2 tbsp) vegetable oil
60 ml (4 tbsp) red wine
120 ml (8 tbsp) balsamic vinegar
45 ml (3 tbsp) grated fresh root ginger
10 ml (2 tsp) paprika
10 ml (2 tsp) cayenne
Salt and ground black pepper

Mix the marinade ingredients together in a shallow glass dish. Add the cubed beef and toss to coat evenly. Cover and refrigerate for 2-3 hours or overnight.

Halve and remove the cores and seeds from the peppers. Cut the peppers into 2.5-cm (1-inch) cubes.

Remove the beef from the marinade, reserving the marinade for basting. Thread the beef, peppers and cherry tomatoes on to the skewers. Cook the kebabs on a prepared barbecue for 10-12 minutes, turning and basting them while they are cooking. SERVES 4

TOP: Barbecued Artichokes
BOTTOM: Lamb & Apricot Skewers,
Spicy Beef Kebabs

AROMATIC BARBECUES

The blends of herbs and spices used in the recipes in this chapter evoke the warmth of the Mediterranean. Chicken Bagna Cauda combines the classic Southern Italian ingredients of anchovies, sun-dried tomatoes, garlic and olive oil, while the Eastern Mediterranean Kofta Kebabs use mint, garlic, cumin and coriander to reproduce the aromatic flavours of that region. Sage, thyme, rosemary, saffron, cayenne and peppercorns are used liberally in the recipes to produce enticing aromas guaranteed to whet most appetites.

SURF & TURF GRILL

450 g (1 lb) fillet steak, cut into 2.5-cm
(1-inch) cubes
8 medium scallops
8 raw tiger prawns, shelled but with tails left intact
4 long metal skewers
Herby rice and salad, to serve (optional)

MARINADE
60 ml (4 tbsp) corn oil
60 ml (4 tbsp) Bourbon whiskey
Grated zest and juice of 2 limes
Salt and ground black pepper

Place the marinade ingredients in a shallow glass dish and mix well. Add the steak, scallops and prawns to the marinade, cover and refrigerate for 4 hours.

Remove the marinated food from the marinade, reserving the marinade for basting, and thread the steak, scallops and prawns on to the skewers.

Cook the skewers on a prepared barbecue for 8-10 minutes, basting them while they are cooking. Serve with herby rice and a salad, if desired.   SERVES 4

BLACKENED SEA BASS

4 sea bass fillets, weighing 150 g (5 oz) each
50 g (2 oz) butter, melted
Lemon wedges, to serve
Skewered New Potatoes, to serve (see page 74)

SPICE MIX
5 ml (1 tsp) salt
5 ml (1 tsp) garlic granules
5 ml (1 tsp) dried parsley
5 ml (1 tsp) chilli powder
2.5 ml (½ tsp) ground bay leaves
15 ml (1 tbsp) cayenne
Ground black pepper

BUTTER SAUCE
45 ml (3 tbsp) dry white wine
30 ml (2 tbsp) white wine vinegar
50 g (2 oz) butter, cubed
150 ml (¼ pint) double cream
15 ml (1 tbsp) chopped fresh parsley
15 ml (1 tbsp) snipped fresh chives

Mix the spice mix ingredients together and place on a plate. Brush the sea bass fillets all over with melted butter, then place on the spice mix and turn to coat evenly. Cover and refrigerate the fillets for 1 hour.

Cook the fish on the oiled rack of a prepared barbecue for 3-4 minutes on each side.

Just before serving, make the sauce. Place the wine and vinegar in a saucepan and boil rapidly for 1-2 minutes to reduce it by half. Then whisk in the butter, a cube at a time, over a low heat. Add the cream and whisk for 1-2 minutes. Stir in the herbs and serve with the sea bass, lemon and potatoes.   SERVES 4

RIGHT: Blackened Sea Bass

SEAFOOD BROCHETTES

350 g (12 oz) skinless, boneless salmon steak
350 g (12 oz) skinless, boneless monkfish
16 large raw prawns
8 metal skewers

CHERVIL MARINADE
60 ml (4 tbsp) sunflower oil
120 ml (8 tbsp) chopped fresh chervil
Salt and ground black pepper

SAFFRON SAUCE
15 ml (1 tbsp) sunflower oil
2 shallots, finely chopped
600 ml (1 pint) dry white wine
Scant 2.5 ml (½ tsp) saffron strands, soaked in
30 ml (2 tbsp) boiling water
300 ml (½ pint) single cream
30 ml (2 tbsp) chopped fresh chervil
30 ml (2 tbsp) snipped fresh chives
Salt and ground black pepper

Cut the salmon and monkfish into 16 chunks each. Place the fish and prawns in a shallow glass dish. Mix the marinade ingredients together and pour over. Toss to coat evenly, cover and refrigerate for 2 hours.

Make the Saffron Sauce. Heat the oil in a saucepan and sauté the shallots for 3 minutes. Add the wine and saffron with the water, bring to the boil and boil steadily for 10-12 minutes, until liquid has reduced to about one-quarter of its original amount. Add the cream and reduce again for 4-5 minutes. Add the herbs and seasoning and heat for a further 30 seconds. Set aside.

Remove the fish and prawns from the marinade, reserving the marinade for basting, and divide them equally between the skewers. Cook on the oiled rack of a prepared barbecue for 8-10 minutes, turning and brushing with marinade. Reheat the sauce and serve it at once with the brochettes. SERVES 4

CRUMBED OYSTERS WITH PIQUANT TOMATO DIP

16 fresh oysters
50 g (2 oz) butter
65 g (2½ oz) fresh white breadcrumbs
2 spring onions, finely chopped
15 ml (1 tbsp) chopped fresh thyme
Generous pinch of paprika
Salt and ground black pepper

PIQUANT TOMATO DIP
450 g (1 lb) tomatoes, roughly chopped
4 spring onions, finely chopped
20 ml (4 tsp) horseradish sauce
10 ml (2 tsp) Worcestershire sauce
5 ml (1 tsp) sugar
Few drops Tabasco sauce
Salt and ground black pepper

Prepare the tomato dip. Place the tomatoes in a food processor and blend briefly to produce a thick purée. Transfer the tomatoes to a saucepan, add the remaining ingredients and bring to the boil. Boil steadily for about 10 minutes to produce a thick sauce. Taste and adjust seasoning, if necessary, and set aside.

Open the oysters, leaving them on the half shell. Melt the butter in a frying pan, add the breadcrumbs and cook for 1 minute. Stir in the remaining ingredients and cook for 3-4 minutes, stirring constantly.

Top each oyster with a little of the crispy breadcrumb mixture, making sure the coating covers the oysters. Cook the oysters on a prepared barbecue for 4-5 minutes, until the oysters are lightly cooked and heated through. Reheat the tomato dip and serve it with the oysters. SERVES 4 AS A STARTER

TOP: Crumbed Oysters with Piquant
Tomato Dip
BOTTOM: Seafood Brochettes

CAJUN TURKEY KEBABS

550 g (1¼ lb) turkey breast, cut into 2.5-cm
(1-inch) cubes
8 wooden or metal skewers
8 baby sweetcorn, blanched for 1 minute
8 shallots, blanched for 5 minutes and peeled
1 large green pepper, cored, seeded and chopped
16 bay leaves
30 ml (2 tbsp) corn oil
Saffron rice, to serve

MARINADE
1 small onion, chopped
2 cloves garlic, chopped
15 ml (1 tbsp) chopped fresh oregano
15 ml (1 tbsp) chopped fresh thyme
7.5 ml (1½ tsp) paprika
2.5 ml (½ tsp) cayenne
Juice of ½ lemon
60 ml (4 tbsp) corn oil
Salt and ground black pepper

Place the marinade ingredients in a food processor and blend to a smooth paste. Pour the marinade into a glass bowl and add the cubed turkey, turning to coat well. Cover and refrigerate for 4 hours.

Thread the marinated turkey on to the skewers, alternating with the sweetcorn, shallots, peppers and bay leaves.

Add the corn oil to the remaining marinade in the dish and brush over the kebabs while cooking them.

Cook the kebabs on a prepared, medium-hot barbecue for about 7 minutes on each side, brushing them with the reserved marinade. Serve at once with the saffron rice.　　　SERVES 4

CREOLE-STYLE PORK SKEWERS

550 g (1¼ lb) pork tenderloin, cut into 24 pieces
8 wooden or metal skewers
1 large red onion, cut into 8 wedges
1 large yellow pepper, cored, seeded and cut
into chunks

MARINADE
60 ml (4 tbsp) olive oil
30 ml (2 tbsp) sun-dried tomato paste
30 ml (2 tbsp) tomato ketchup
30 ml (2 tbsp) lemon juice
2 cloves garlic, crushed
2 small pickled green chillies, chopped
Salt and ground black pepper

Mix all the marinade ingredients together. Pour the marinade into a shallow glass dish and add the pork pieces, turning to coat well. Cover and refrigerate for 4 hours.

Remove the pork from the marinade, reserving the marinade for basting, and thread the pork on to the skewers with the onions and peppers.

Cook the pork skewers on a prepared, medium-hot barbecue for 12-15 minutes, basting them with the reserved marinade while they are cooking.　　SERVES 4

RIGHT: Cajun Turkey Kebabs

CHICKEN PINWHEELS

4 skinless, boneless chicken breasts, weighing
150 g (5 oz) each
100-g (4-oz) piece leek, cut into 2 lengths
45 ml (3 tbsp) olive oil for brushing
Rice, to serve (optional)

STUFFING

25 g (I oz) pistachio nuts, finely chopped
25 g (I oz) fresh white breadcrumbs
50 g (2 oz) butter, melted
24 basil leaves, torn
Salt and ground black pepper

BASIL CREAM SAUCE

300 ml (½ pint) single cream
16 large basil leaves, torn
Ground black pepper

Place the stuffing ingredients in a bowl and mix well.

Place a chicken breast between two pieces of grease-proof paper and pound with a rolling pin or mallet to flatten. Repeat with the remaining chicken breasts.

Blanch the leeks for 3 minutes, then drain and refresh in cold water. Slice each piece of leek in half lengthways. Dry the pieces of leek on kitchen paper.

Spread one-quarter of the stuffing on to each chicken breast, leaving a 1.5-cm (½-inch) border around the edges. Place a piece of leek in the centre, then roll up to enclose the stuffing. Secure with string. Repeat with the remaining chicken. Refrigerate for 2 hours.

Brush the pinwheels with a little olive oil and cook on a prepared barbecue for 20-25 minutes, turning and brushing them with more oil as they cook.

Make the sauce. Place the cream, basil and seasoning in a saucepan and bring to the boil. Boil rapidly for 4-5 minutes, until the sauce has reduced slightly. To serve, slice the chicken pinwheels thickly and serve with some sauce and rice. SERVES 4

CHICKEN BAGNA CAUDA

4 boneless chicken breasts with skin, weighing about
175 g (6 oz) each
60 ml (4 tbsp) chopped fresh parsley
60 ml (4 tbsp) olive oil
4 cloves garlic, crushed
Salt and ground black pepper
Polenta or pasta, to serve (optional)

ANCHOVY SAUCE

240 ml (8 fl oz) olive oil
4 cloves garlic, crushed
8 anchovy fillets, finely chopped
12 halves sun-dried tomatoes in oil, drained and finely chopped
30 ml (2 tbsp) chilli sauce
30 ml (2 tbsp) chopped fresh parsley
Ground black pepper

Make several deep slashes through the skin and flesh of each chicken breast. Mix the chopped parsley, oil, garlic and seasoning together. Work this mixture into the slashes and over the surface of each chicken breast. Place the chicken in a shallow dish, pour over any remaining mixture, cover and refrigerate for 2 hours.

Make the sauce. Heat the oil in a saucepan and sauté the garlic for I minute. Add the remaining ingredients and simmer gently for 3-4 minutes. Set the sauce aside until required.

Remove the chicken from the dish, reserving any remaining mixture for basting. Cook the chicken breasts on a prepared barbecue for about 20 minutes, turning and basting occasionally. Test the chicken with a skewer: if juices run clear, the chicken is cooked.

Reheat the sauce and serve it with the cooked chicken and the cooked polenta or pasta. SERVES 4

TOP: Chicken Pinwheels
BOTTOM: Chicken Bagna Cauda

AROMATIC DUCK BREASTS WITH PORT & CHERRIES

4 duck breasts, weighing 200 g (7 oz) each
New potatoes, to serve (optional)

MARINADE
60 ml (4 tbsp) chopped fresh rosemary
20 ml (4 tsp) ground cinnamon
10 ml (2 tsp) ground allspice
5 ml (1 tsp) soft brown sugar
45 ml (3 tbsp) vegetable oil

PORT AND CHERRY SAUCE
360 ml (12 fl oz) ruby port
120 ml (8 tbsp) red wine vinegar
20 ml (4 tsp) soft brown sugar
225 g (8 oz) fresh cherries, halved, or
175 g (6 oz) stoned whole canned cherries
Salt and ground black pepper

Make several deep slashes through the skin and flesh of each duck breast. Mix the marinade ingredients together and work this mixture into the slashes and surface of the duck breasts. Cover and refrigerate for at least 2 hours.

Make the sauce. Place the port, vinegar and sugar in a saucepan and bring to the boil. Boil the sauce for 4-5 minutes to reduce it, then add the cherries. Reduce the heat and cook very gently for a further 6-8 minutes. Taste and adjust seasoning, if necessary, and set the sauce aside until required.

Cook the duck breasts on a prepared, medium-hot barbecue for about 10 minutes on each side, until cooked through. Reheat the sauce. Slice the duck breasts and serve them with the Port and Cherry Sauce and potatoes, if desired.   SERVES 4

BBQ DUCK WITH SAGE & ORANGE STUFFING

4 leg portions of duck

SAGE AND ORANGE STUFFING
60 ml (4 tbsp) butter, softened
10 ml (2 tsp) dry mustard powder
60 ml (4 tbsp) very finely chopped celery
8 sage leaves, chopped
Grated zest of 1 large orange
Salt and ground black pepper

MARINADE
Juice of 1 large orange
2 sage leaves, chopped
60 ml (4 tbsp) orange marmalade
15 ml (1 tbsp) vegetable oil

Mix the ingredients for the stuffing together in a bowl. Loosen the skin of the duck portions by easing it away from the leg meat. Divide the stuffing between the duck portions, placing it between the skin and leg meat, and spreading it out as much as possible.

Mix together the marinade ingredients. Place the duck portions in a shallow glass dish, pour over the marinade, then cover and refrigerate for at least 2 hours or overnight.

Remove the duck from the marinade, reserving the marinade for basting. Cook the duck on a prepared barbecue for 20-25 minutes, turning and basting the duck while it is cooking. Serve at once.   SERVES 4

TOP: Aromatic Duck Breasts with
Port & Cherries
BOTTOM: BBQ Duck with Sage &
Orange Stuffing

KOFTA KEBABS

350 g (12 oz) minced lamb
4 slices crustless white bread, crumbled
1 onion, finely chopped
4 cloves garlic, crushed
60 ml (4 tbsp) chopped fresh mint
30 ml (2 tbsp) chopped fresh parsley
60 ml (4 tbsp) pine nuts, toasted
30 ml (2 tbsp) raisins
30 ml (2 tbsp) cumin seeds, lightly toasted
5 ml (1 tsp) ground coriander
1 egg, beaten
Salt and ground black pepper
4 metal skewers
Oil for brushing
50 g (2 oz) iceberg lettuce, shredded
2 tomatoes, cut into wedges
1 onion, sliced
12 black olives
Warm pitta bread and lemon wedges, to serve

MINT DRESSING

160 ml (5½ fl oz) Greek-style yoghurt
60 ml (4 tbsp) chopped fresh mint
Pinch of cayenne
Salt and ground black pepper

Place the first 12 ingredients in a food processor and process briefly to combine. Divide the mixture into 12 portions and shape each portion into an oval-shaped patty. Refrigerate for 2 hours.

Mix the Mint Dressing ingredients together in a bowl and refrigerate until required.

Thread three koftas on to each skewer and brush with a little oil. Cook on a prepared barbecue for 6 minutes on each side, turning and brushing with oil.

Divide the lettuce, tomato, onion and olives between four plates. Add the kebabs and serve at once with the dressing, pitta and lemon.   SERVES 4

PEPPERED STEAKS WITH HERB COUS-COUS

4 fillet steaks, weighing 150 g (5 oz) each
20 ml (4 tsp) olive oil
60 ml (4 tbsp) tropical peppercorns, crushed

HERB COUS-COUS

175 g (6 oz) cous-cous
480 ml (16 fl oz) boiling water
30 ml (2 tbsp) olive oil
4 spring onions, finely chopped
120 ml (8 tbsp) chopped fresh parsley
Finely grated zest of 1 large lemon
20 ml (4 tsp) lemon juice
1 red pepper, grilled, skinned and diced
Salt and ground black pepper

Brush each steak with a little olive oil and press the crushed peppercorns on to the surfaces.

Place the cous-cous in a bowl with a little salt and pour over the boiling water. Leave the cous-cous to stand for 5-10 minutes, until the water has been absorbed and the grains have swelled up.

Cook the peppered steaks on the oiled rack of a prepared barbecue for about 5 minutes on each side, turning them halfway through cooking.

Just before serving, finish the cous-cous by heating the oil in a large saucepan, adding the cous-cous and all the remaining ingredients, and stirring to combine and heat through. Serve the peppered steaks with the cous-cous.   SERVES 4

RIGHT: Kofta Kebabs

BBQ VEAL ROLLS

4 veal escalopes, weighing 150 g (5 oz) each
50 g (2 oz) fresh spinach
15 ml (1 tbsp) olive oil
2 large cloves garlic, chopped
30 ml (2 tbsp) finely chopped red onion
100 g (4 oz) ricotta cheese
20 ml (4 tsp) pine nuts, toasted
Salt and ground black pepper
Barbecued Artichokes, to serve (see page 36)

MARINADE
90 ml (6 tbsp) white wine
45 ml (3 tbsp) olive oil
Pinch of nutmeg
Ground black pepper

Place a veal escalope between two pieces of grease-proof paper and pound with a rolling pin or mallet to flatten. Repeat with the remaining veal escalopes.

Steam the spinach, then lay the leaves on kitchen paper to remove any excess moisture. Heat the oil in a saucepan, add the garlic and onion and sauté for 1-2 minutes until soft. Transfer to a large bowl and stir in the ricotta cheese, pine nuts and seasoning.

Season a veal escalope, then place one-quarter of the spinach in a layer over the veal, leaving a 1.5-cm (½-inch) border around the edges. Season again and spread one-quarter of the ricotta mixture over the spinach. Roll the veal escalope up to completely enclose the filling. Secure with string. Repeat with the remaining veal, spinach and ricotta mixture.

Place the marinade ingredients in a shallow glass dish and mix well. Add the veal rolls to the dish and turn to coat evenly. Cover and refrigerate for 2 hours.

Remove the veal rolls from the marinade, reserving the marinade for basting. Cook on a prepared barbecue for about 20 minutes, turning and basting. Serve at once with Barbecued Artichokes.　　　　SERVES 4

PECAN NUT TURKEY ESCALOPES

4 turkey escalopes, weighing 100 g (4 oz) each
30 ml (2 tbsp) Dijon mustard
30 ml (2 tbsp) soured cream
100 g (4 oz) pecan nuts, coarsely ground
Oil for brushing
Lemon wedges, to serve

SOURED CREAM DIP
90 ml (6 tbsp) soured cream
30 ml (2 tbsp) snipped fresh chives
10 ml (2 tsp) Dijon mustard
Lemon juice to taste
Salt and ground black pepper

Place the turkey escalopes between two pieces of greaseproof paper and pound them with a rolling pin or mallet to flatten.

Mix together the Dijon mustard and soured cream and place the ground pecans on a flat plate. Dip an escalope in the mustard mixture and then place it on the plate of pecans and turn to coat evenly. Repeat with the remaining turkey escalopes. Cover and refrigerate for at least 2 hours before barbecuing.

Mix the ingredients for the dip together, cover and refrigerate until required.

Brush the pecan-coated turkey escalopes with a little oil and cook them on a prepared barbecue for 6-7 minutes on each side, until they are golden and cooked through. Serve hot with lemon wedges and the Soured Cream Dip.　　　　SERVES 4

TOP: Pecan Nut Turkey Escalopes
BOTTOM: BBQ Veal Rolls

VEGETABLE BARBECUES

Recipes for starters, side dishes and main courses are included in this chapter, enabling you to create a totally vegetarian meal, if so desired. Although some of the recipes would not immediately be associated with barbecues, they work very well. For example, the Savoy Cabbage Parcels and the Vine Leaves with Feta, Olives & Tomato are novel barbecue ideas, but delicious. Some recipes will require a little extra care with handling, as the ingredients are more fragile than traditional barbecue ingredients.

SPICED CORN ON THE COB

4 corn on the cob, husks removed
30 ml (2 tbsp) olive oil
2.5 ml (½ tsp) cayenne
Salt and ground black pepper

CHILLI BUTTER
75 g (3 oz) butter, softened
30 ml (2 tbsp) coarsely chopped fresh coriander
10 ml (2 tsp) finely chopped fresh red chilli
Salt and ground black pepper

Prepare the Chilli Butter. Mix the ingredients together until thoroughly combined. Place the butter in a sausage shape on a piece of cling film or greaseproof paper. Roll up to form a cylinder and refrigerate to harden the butter.

Cook the corn in plenty of boiling, salted water for about 15 minutes, until it is tender. Drain, then toss the corn in the olive oil, cayenne and seasoning to coat.

Cook the corn on a prepared barbecue for 10-15 minutes, turning occasionally while cooking. They are ready to serve when they are slightly charred. Serve at once with discs of Chilli Butter. SERVES 4

MEDITERRANEAN VEGETABLES

The quantity of herb oil in this recipe is sufficient to cook the vegetables listed below. Vegetables may be varied according to preference.

4 corn on the cob
8 baby fennel bulbs
4 plum tomatoes
2 red onions
2 peppers, any colour

HERB AND GARLIC OIL
150 ml (¼ pint) extra virgin olive oil
30 ml (2 tbsp) balsamic vinegar
2 cloves garlic, crushed
120 ml (8 tbsp) chopped fresh mixed herbs, such as fennel fronds, chives, parsley and basil
Salt and ground black pepper

Prepare the vegetables for barbecuing. Peel back the husks from the corn and knot them at the base. Remove all the threads from the sweetcorn and discard. Trim the baby fennel and halve the tomatoes. Halve the onions, leaving the skins intact. Halve the peppers lengthways and remove the cores and seeds, leaving the stalks intact.

Mix the ingredients for the Herb and Garlic Oil together. To cook the vegetables, brush them liberally with the herb oil and cook on a prepared barbecue, turning and brushing frequently until they are cooked through and slightly charred. The corn on the cob will take about 20 minutes to cook, the onions 15-20 minutes, and the fennel, tomatoes and peppers about 10 minutes. SERVES 4-6

RIGHT: Mediterranean Vegetables

52

HALLOUMI, COURGETTE & MUSHROOM SKEWERS

These cheese and vegetable skewers make a satisfying vegetarian main course when served with a tomato and olive salad and warm pitta bread.

350 g (12 oz) halloumi cheese
1 red pepper, halved, cored and seeded
175 g (6 oz) courgettes, cut into 8 chunks
8 large mushrooms, halved
120 ml (8 tbsp) extra virgin olive oil
30 ml (2 tbsp) chopped fresh thyme
2 cloves garlic, chopped
Ground black pepper
8 wooden or metal skewers

Cut the cheese and red pepper into 2.5-cm (1-inch) squares. Place them in a shallow dish with the courgettes and mushrooms. Mix the olive oil, thyme, garlic and pepper together and pour over the vegetables. Toss gently to coat evenly, then thread the cheese and vegetables on the skewers. Brush with any remaining oil mixture.

Cook on the oiled rack of a prepared barbecue for about 8 minutes, turning occasionally and brushing with any remaining oil mixture. The skewers are ready to serve when the cheese is golden and the vegetables are tender. SERVES 4

SPICY POTATO, SHALLOT & FENNEL KEBABS

Baby fennel bulbs are used in this recipe, but if they are unavailable, substitute small wedges of fennel.

24 baby new potatoes
8 small shallots
16 baby fennel bulbs, about 275 g (10 oz) in total weight
20 ml (4 tsp) mustard seeds
20 ml (4 tsp) cumin seeds
20 ml (4 tsp) garam masala
10 ml (2 tsp) turmeric
20 ml (4 tsp) lemon juice
120 ml (8 tbsp) groundnut oil
Salt and ground black pepper
8 wooden or metal skewers

Cook the potatoes in boiling, salted water for about 12 minutes until tender. Drain and transfer to a large mixing bowl. Cook the shallots in boiling water for 4 minutes, drain and, when cool enough to handle, peel them. Add to the potatoes, along with the fennel.

Crush the mustard and cumin seeds lightly and place them in a bowl with the garam masala, turmeric, lemon juice, groundnut oil and some seasoning. Mix to combine, then pour over the prepared vegetables and toss to coat well. Cover and refrigerate for 2 hours, if time permits.

Remove the vegetables from the mixture, reserving any remaining mixture for basting, and thread the vegetables evenly between the skewers. Cook the kebabs on a prepared barbecue for about 12 minutes, turning and basting while cooking. SERVES 4

TOP: Spicy Potato, Shallot & Fennel Kebabs
BOTTOM: Halloumi, Courgette & Mushroom Skewers

GRILLED VEGETABLES WITH TAHINI DRESSING

350 g (12 oz) sweet potato, peeled and cut
into 4 slices
450 g (1 lb) celeriac, peeled and cut into 4 slices
350 g (12 oz) pumpkin, peeled and cut
into 4 wedges
2 medium parsnips, peeled and halved lengthways
90 ml (6 tbsp) olive oil for brushing
Sea salt and ground black pepper

TAHINI DRESSING
60 ml (4 tbsp) light tahini
60 ml (4 tbsp) mayonnaise
45 ml (3 tbsp) olive oil
1.25 ml (¼ tsp) paprika
2 cloves garlic, crushed
2 spring onions, chopped
10 ml (2 tsp) lemon juice
Salt and ground black pepper

Mix the ingredients for the dressing together in a bowl
and refrigerate until required.

Cook the different types of root vegetables in-
dividually in boiling, salted water until they are just
tender. The celeriac will take about 12 minutes to
cook, the sweet potato 10 minutes, the parsnip 8
minutes and the pumpkin 6 minutes.

Drain the cooked vegetables and dry them on
kitchen paper. Brush them all over with olive oil and
season generously with salt and pepper.

Cook the vegetables on the oiled rack of a prepared
barbecue for about 6 minutes on each side, turning
them halfway through cooking and brushing occasionally with oil. Serve the barbecued vegetables with the
Tahini Dressing.   SERVES 4

CHARGRILLED YAMS & PLANTAINS WITH HOT PEPPER MAYONNAISE

*Green, unripe plantains can be substituted for the
half-ripe plantains in this recipe, but they will take
longer to cook.*

4 × 150-g (5-oz) slices yam, peeled
4 × 75-g (3-oz) thick slices half-ripe plantain, with
skins left intact
Corn oil for brushing
Salt and ground black pepper

HOT PEPPER MAYONNAISE
90 ml (6 tbsp) mayonnaise
30 ml (2 tbsp) chopped fresh thyme
5 ml (1 tsp) seeded and finely chopped hot
Jamaican chilli
20 ml (4 tsp) freshly squeezed lime juice
Salt and ground black pepper

Cook the yam slices in boiling, salted water for 15
minutes or until tender. Drain and set aside until required. Mix the mayonnaise ingredients together and
refrigerate until required.

Brush the yam and plantain slices all over with corn
oil and season with salt and pepper. Cook on a prepared barbecue, turning occasionally until they are
tender and charred on the outside. The yams will be
ready to serve in 15 minutes and the plantains in about
12 minutes. Serve at once with the Hot Pepper
Mayonnaise.   SERVES 4 AS A STARTER

TOP: Chargrilled Yams & Plantains with Hot
Pepper Mayonnaise
BOTTOM: Grilled Vegetables with
Tahini Dressing

SAVOY CABBAGE PARCELS

These cabbage parcels make an excellent accompaniment to barbecued pork or chicken.

4 large Savoy or pointed green cabbage leaves
75 g (3 oz) butter
100 g (4 oz) leeks, thinly sliced
100 g (4 oz) carrots, peeled and coarsely grated
175 g (6 oz) cooked brown basmati rice
25 g (1 oz) pumpkin seeds, lightly toasted
30 ml (2 tbsp) chopped fresh tarragon
Salt and ground black pepper

Cut away the tough stalks from the cabbage leaves, then blanch the leaves in boiling, salted water for 1-2 minutes until they are just tender. Drain and refresh in cold water, then lay cabbage leaves on kitchen paper to dry them.

Melt 50 g (2 oz) of the butter in a pan, add the leeks and sauté for 3 minutes. Stir in the carrot and sauté for a further minute. Remove pan from the heat and stir in the rice, pumpkin seeds, tarragon and seasoning.

Lay a cabbage leaf on a large piece of foil and place one-quarter of the rice mixture in the centre. Fold the cabbage around the filling to form a parcel, dot with one-quarter of the remaining butter and fold up the foil to enclose the cabbage. Repeat with the remaining cabbage leaves and filling.

Cook the foil parcels on a prepared barbecue for 13-15 minutes, until the cabbage is tender and the filling heated through.   SERVES 4

VINE LEAVES WITH FETA, OLIVES & TOMATO

8 large vacuum-packed vine leaves
30 ml (2 tbsp) olive oil
100 g (4 oz) feta cheese, cut into small cubes
16 small black olives
8 cherry tomatoes, halved
8 sprigs fresh oregano
Ground black pepper
Cocktail sticks
Greek-style sesame bread, to serve (optional)

Rinse the vine leaves and dry them on kitchen paper. Lay them on a flat surface and brush each leaf with a little olive oil.

Divide the feta, black olives, tomatoes and oregano evenly between the leaves, placing them in the centre of each leaf. Grind over some black pepper and fold the leaves around the filling to enclose it completely. Secure the vine leaf parcels with cocktail sticks.

Brush the outside of the parcels with the remaining oil and cook them on a prepared barbecue for about 4-5 minutes, until the cheese has begun to melt. They do not need to be turned, but do keep the skewered side of the parcels upright, away from the coals.

Serve two vine leaves to each person. Peel away the leaves and eat the filling. The leaves are purely to enclose the filling and are not meant to be eaten. Serve with sesame bread, if desired.

SERVES 4 AS A STARTER

RIGHT: Vine Leaves with Feta, Olives & Tomato

PATTY PAN, ONION & AUBERGINE KEBABS

16 small patty pan squash
8 baby aubergines, halved lengthways
8 baby onions, unpeeled
8 wooden or metal skewers

MARINADE
60 ml (4 tbsp) chopped fresh coriander
120 ml (8 tbsp) olive oil
5 ml (1 tsp) garam masala
5 ml (1 tsp) dried chilli flakes
2 cloves garlic, crushed
Salt and ground black pepper

BULGHUR WHEAT PILAF
225 g (8 oz) bulghur wheat
700 ml (1¼ pints) boiling vegetable stock
60 ml (4 tbsp) olive oil
1 onion, chopped
2 cloves garlic, crushed
5 ml (1 tsp) ground cumin
50 g (2 oz) raisins
60 ml (4 tbsp) coarsely chopped coriander
Salt and ground black pepper

Mix the marinade ingredients together in a large bowl. Boil the patty pan squash for 4 minutes, drain and add to the marinade, along with the aubergines. Boil the onions for 5 minutes, then drain, peel and halve them. Add the onions to the bowl of vegetables. Toss gently to coat evenly. Cover and refrigerate for 2 hours.

Make the pilaf. Soak the bulghur wheat in the boiling stock for about 40 minutes, until the grains have swelled and are tender. Drain well. Heat the oil in a saucepan and sauté the onion, garlic and cumin for 4 minutes until soft. Remove from the heat and stir in the bulghur wheat, raisins and coriander. Season the pilaf generously and set aside until required.

Thread the marinated vegetables evenly between the skewers, reserving the marinade for basting. Cook the kebabs on a prepared barbecue for about 10 minutes, turning and basting occasionally while cooking. Serve at once with the pilaf.   SERVES 4

ORIENTAL TOFU SKEWERS

250 g (9 oz) tofu, cut into 16 cubes
1 large orange pepper, grilled, skinned and cut into 8 long strips
8 cherry tomatoes
75 g (3 oz) broccoli, divided into 8 florets
8 wooden or metal skewers
Noodles, to serve (optional)

SESAME MARINADE
45 ml (3 tbsp) vegetable oil
15 ml (1 tbsp) sesame oil
15 ml (1 tbsp) soy sauce
5 ml (1 tsp) grated fresh root ginger
5 ml (1 tsp) sesame seeds
30 ml (2 tbsp) rice wine vinegar
1 spring onion, finely chopped

Mix the marinade ingredients together in a large bowl. Add the tofu cubes to the marinade, toss gently to coat, cover and refrigerate for 2 hours.

Remove the tofu from the marinade, reserving the remaining marinade for basting. Thread the tofu, pepper strips, tomatoes and broccoli on the skewers.

Cook the skewers on a prepared barbecue for 8-10 minutes, turning and basting them while cooking. Just before serving, pour any remaining marinade over the tofu skewers. Serve with noodles, if desired.
                                        SERVES 4

TOP AND BOTTOM: Oriental Tofu Skewers
CENTRE: Patty Pan, Onion & Aubergine Kebabs

FALAFEL PATTIES WITH YOGHURT & MINT DIP

30 ml (2 tbsp) vegetable oil
5 ml (1 tsp) cumin seeds
1 onion, finely chopped
2 cloves garlic, crushed
5 ml (1 tsp) chopped fresh green chilli
2.5 ml (½ tsp) turmeric
432-g (15-oz) can chick-peas, drained
Salt and ground black pepper
50 g (2 oz) fresh white breadcrumbs
1 egg, beaten
30 ml (2 tbsp) chopped fresh coriander
Flour for coating
Oil for brushing
A barbecue flat griddle plate or wire basket
for cooking
Lemon wedges and pitta bread, to serve

YOGHURT AND MINT DIP
120 ml (8 tbsp) Greek-style yoghurt
60 ml (4 tbsp) chopped fresh mint
5 ml (1 tsp) lemon juice
Pinch of ground cumin
Salt and ground black pepper

Mix the ingredients for the dip together, cover and refrigerate until required.

Heat the vegetable oil in a frying pan, add cumin seeds, onion and garlic and sauté for 5 minutes. Add chilli and turmeric and cook for a further 2 minutes. Transfer the spice mixture to a food processor, add the chick-peas and seasoning, and blend briefly until the chick-peas are roughly mashed and combined with the spices.

Transfer to a bowl and add the breadcrumbs, egg and coriander. Mix to combine and divide into eight portions. With floured hands, shape into patties and refrigerate the falafel for about 4 hours.

Oil the griddle plate and heat on a prepared barbecue or, alternatively, place the falafel in a wire basket. Brush the falafel all over with oil and cook on the barbecue for 6-7 minutes on each side. Serve hot with the dip, lemon and pitta.   SERVES 4

PEPPERS STUFFED WITH NUTTY RICE

4 medium red peppers
Oil for brushing

NUTTY RICE
225 g (8 oz) basmati rice
5 ml (1 tsp) saffron strands infused in
30 ml (2 tbsp) boiling water for 10 minutes
60 ml (4 tbsp) vegetable oil
1 red onion, thinly sliced
4 small cloves garlic, crushed
50 g (2 oz) pine nuts, toasted
25 g (1 oz) pistachio nuts, coarsely chopped
60 ml (4 tbsp) chopped fresh parsley
Salt and ground black pepper

Prepare the Nutty Rice. Cook the basmati rice in boiling, salted water, to which the saffron and its water has been added. The rice will take 8-10 minutes to cook. Drain and place the rice in a mixing bowl.

Heat the oil in a pan and sauté the onion and garlic for 2-3 minutes. Add to the rice, with the pine nuts, pistachios, parsley and seasoning. Toss to combine.

Halve the peppers lengthways and core and seed, leaving the stalks intact. Divide the Nutty Rice between the pepper halves. Lightly oil four large pieces of foil and place two pepper halves on each piece of foil. Fold to produce parcels and cook on a prepared barbecue for about 20 minutes, until the peppers are tender and the rice is hot.   SERVES 4

RIGHT: Falafel Patties with Yoghurt & Mint Dip

MUSHROOM & MOZZARELLA BROCHETTES

Rosemary branches can be used in this recipe to skewer the food. Choose long, mature branches and strip off the leaves, just leaving a few at the top. Soak them in cold water for 1 hour.

16 fresh shiitake mushrooms, about 100 g (4 oz) in total weight
16 button mushrooms, about 225 g (8 oz) in total weight
16 mini mozzarella cheese balls
8 metal or rosemary branch skewers
Steamed cous-cous, to serve (optional)

MARINADE

Zest and juice of 2 small lemons
30 ml (2 tbsp) olive oil
45 ml (3 tbsp) chopped fresh rosemary
10 ml (2 tsp) chilli oil
½ small fresh red chilli, seeded and finely chopped
½ small fresh green chilli, seeded and finely chopped
2 cloves garlic, crushed
Salt and ground black pepper

Mix the marinade ingredients together. Place the two types of mushrooms and the mini mozzarellas in a mixing bowl. Pour over the marinade and toss gently to coat evenly. Cover and refrigerate for 2 hours.

Remove the marinated mushrooms and cheese from the dish, reserving any remaining marinade for basting, and thread the mushrooms and cheese evenly between the skewers or rosemary branches.

Cook the brochettes on a prepared medium-hot barbecue for about 10 minutes, turning and basting them while cooking. Serve at once with steamed cous-cous, if desired.   SERVES 4

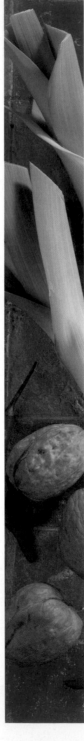

GOAT'S CHEESE, LEEK & WALNUT BRUSCHETTA

6 slices French bread, cut on an acute angle
45 ml (3 tbsp) olive oil
6 × 40-g (1½-oz) slices soft goat's cheese
Ground black pepper

LEEK AND WALNUT TOPPING

30 ml (2 tbsp) olive oil
75 g (3 oz) leeks, thinly sliced
15 g (½ oz) walnuts, coarsely chopped
Salt and ground black pepper

Make the topping. Heat the oil in a saucepan and sauté the leeks for about 3 minutes until they are soft. Remove from the heat and stir in the remaining ingredients. Set aside until required.

Brush both sides of the sliced bread with 30 ml (2 tbsp) of the olive oil. Place the bread on the grill rack of a prepared barbecue and cook for 2-3 minutes, until toasted on one side. Do not toast the other side.

Remove from the barbecue and divide the Leek and Walnut Topping between the toasted sides of the bread slices. Top each with a piece of goat's cheese and drizzle with the remaining olive oil. Grind over some black pepper.

Return the bruschetta to the barbecue and cook for a further 3-4 minutes until the cheese begins to melt. Serve at once.   SERVES 6 AS A STARTER

LEFT AND BOTTOM: Goat's Cheese, Leek & Walnut Bruschetta
RIGHT: Mushroom & Mozzarella Brochettes

SWEET DESSERTS

The recipes in this chapter allow you to extend your barbecue meal to the last course (provided that the coals have been tended so they are still glowing). Fruits lend themselves to barbecuing, as they cook quickly and combine well with other flavours. Barbecued bananas are a classic favourite and here made more special by adding a maple syrup and pecan nut sauce. Tamarillos with Brown Sugar are extremely easy to prepare, yet produce a delicious and unusual dessert. For a more sophisticated dish, try Almond-stuffed Medjool Dates, which are steeped in cinnamon and brandy.

BANANAS WITH MAPLE SYRUP & PECAN NUTS

50 g (2 oz) pecan nuts, coarsely chopped
90 ml (6 tbsp) maple syrup
4 bananas
Vanilla or rum-and-raisin ice cream, to serve

Place the chopped pecans and maple syrup in a small saucepan and set aside until required.

Cook the whole bananas in their skins on a prepared barbecue for 12-15 minutes, until the skins are completely black and the bananas are soft.

Just before serving, gently warm the pecan nuts and maple syrup. To serve, remove the bananas from their skins and top with the warm nutty syrup and scoops of ice cream. SERVES 4

FRUIT SKEWERS WITH CHOCOLATE-NUT SAUCE

12 strawberries
6 apricots, halved
3 pears, peeled and cut into quarters
30 ml (2 tbsp) caster sugar
6 wooden or metal skewers

CHOCOLATE-NUT SAUCE
100 g (4 oz) milk chocolate, chopped
150 ml (¼ pint) single cream
6 marshmallows, chopped
25 g (1 oz) skinless hazelnuts, toasted and chopped

Make the sauce by melting the chocolate, cream and marshmallows gently, stirring constantly. Then whisk to produce a smooth sauce and boil for 2 minutes to thicken. Stir in the nuts and set the sauce aside.

Place the fruit in a bowl, sprinkle over the caster sugar and toss gently to coat. Divide the fruit between the skewers.

Place the fruit skewers on a prepared barbecue and cook them for 5-6 minutes, turning frequently, until the fruit is warmed through. Serve the skewers at once with the Chocolate-Nut Sauce passed separately for dipping. SERVES 6

RIGHT: Fruit Skewers with Chocolate-Nut Sauce

EXOTIC FRUIT WITH PASSIONFRUIT DIP

I small ripe pawpaw, cut into 4 thick slices with seeds removed
I small ripe mango, cut into quarters around the stone
2 bananas, unpeeled and halved lengthways
2 thick slices pineapple, halved
50 g (2 oz) unsalted butter, melted
10 ml (2 tsp) sifted icing sugar

PASSIONFRUIT DIP
200 ml (7 fl oz) crème fraîche
15 ml (1 tbsp) sifted icing sugar
Pulp and juice of 3 passionfruit
Mint sprigs, to decorate

Mix the ingredients for the dip together in a bowl. Cover and refrigerate until required.

Place all the fruit on a large tray. Mix together the melted butter and icing sugar, and brush the mixture all over the fruit. Cook all the fruit on a prepared barbecue, turning the pawpaw, mango and pineapple over occasionally until they begin to caramelize. The mango, pineapple and bananas will take about 6 minutes to cook, and the pawpaw about 4 minutes. Garnish with mint and serve the fruit with the dip.

SERVES 4

PEACH & ALMOND DESSERT WITH AMARETTO

50 g (2 oz) Madeira cake, crumbled
6 amaretti biscuits, coarsely crushed
60 ml (4 tbsp) Amaretto liqueur
4 ripe peaches, halved with stones removed
25 g (1 oz) flaked almonds, toasted
120 ml (8 tbsp) freshly squeezed orange juice
Mascarpone cheese, to serve

Mix the Madeira cake, amaretti biscuits and half the Amaretto liqueur together in a bowl. Divide the mixture between the hollows of the peaches. Sprinkle a few flaked almonds on to each peach half.

Mix the remaining Amaretto liqueur and the orange juice together. Place two peach halves on a large piece of foil. Spoon over one-quarter of the orange juice mixture and fold over the foil to make a parcel. Repeat with the remaining peaches to produce four parcels.

Cook the peach parcels on a prepared barbecue for about 10 minutes, until they are tender and warmed through. Serve with mascarpone cheese.   SERVES 4

TOP: Peach & Almond Dessert with Amaretto
BOTTOM: Exotic Fruit with Passionfruit Dip

ALMOND-STUFFED MEDJOOL DATES

12 large fresh Medjool dates
75 g (3 oz) blanched almonds, toasted
30 ml (2 tbsp) mascarpone cheese or cream cheese
60 ml (4 tbsp) brandy
2 cinnamon sticks, broken in half
30 ml (2 tbsp) soft brown sugar
60 ml (4 tbsp) freshly squeezed orange juice
Greek yoghurt, to serve (optional)

Make a slit in the side of each date and remove and discard the stones.

Reserve 12 whole blanched almonds and chop the rest finely. Place them in a bowl and add the mascarpone cheese and half the brandy. Mix well to combine and fill the dates with the mixture, adding a whole almond to each cavity.

Place six dates on a large piece of foil and place a cinnamon stick on the foil with the dates. Mix the remaining brandy, brown sugar and orange juice together. Spoon half of the mixture over the dates. Wrap up the foil to produce a parcel. Repeat with the remaining dates, cinnamon and orange juice mixture.

Cook the foil parcels on a prepared barbecue for about 10 minutes, until the dates are tender and warmed through. Serve with yoghurt, if desired.

SERVES 4

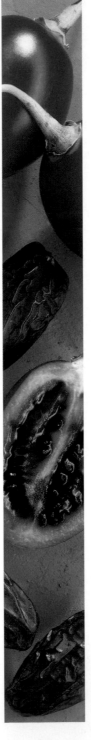

TAMARILLOS WITH BROWN SUGAR

4 ripe tamarillos (tree tomatoes)
45 ml (3 tbsp) Demerara sugar
Vanilla ice cream, to serve

Halve the tamarillos and place two halves on a piece of foil. Sprinkle with one-quarter of the Demerara sugar and fold the foil over to produce a parcel. Repeat with the remaining tamarillos and sugar to produce four individual parcels.

Cook the tamarillo parcels on a prepared barbecue for about 10 minutes, until they are warmed through and the sugar has melted. Serve at once with scoops of vanilla ice cream.

SERVES 4

TOP LEFT: Tamarillos with Brown Sugar
BOTTOM: Almond-stuffed Medjool Dates

ACCOMPANIMENTS

The collection of recipes in this chapter will help you provide a complete barbecue meal. Some of the accompaniments, such as Skewered New Potatoes and Olive, Basil & Parmesan Ciabatta, are actually cooked on the barbecue. Other recipes include rice and salad dishes, muffins and the classic Chilli Beans. Although these are not cooked on the barbecue, they are quick and easy to prepare and make good accompaniments to many of the recipes in the book.

JASMINE & SESAME RICE

225 g (8 oz) Thai jasmine rice or fragrant rice
5 ml (1 tsp) sesame oil
30 ml (2 tbsp) sesame seeds, toasted
4 spring onions, finely chopped
60 ml (4 tbsp) chopped fresh coriander
10 ml (2 tsp) lime juice
Salt and ground black pepper

Cook the rice in boiling, salted water for about 10 minutes, or until it is tender. Drain and transfer the rice to a large bowl.

Add the remaining ingredients to the warm rice and stir gently to mix. Taste and adjust seasoning, if necessary, and serve at once.   SERVES 4

SPICY RICE

225 g (8 oz) mixed wild and long-grain rice
45 ml (3 tbsp) olive oil
3 cloves garlic, crushed
5 ml (1 tsp) dried chilli flakes
45 ml (3 tbsp) chopped fresh parsley
175 g (6 oz) sweetcorn kernels
Salt and ground black pepper

Cook the rice in boiling, salted water for about 10 minutes, or until the rice is tender. Drain and set it aside. Heat the oil in a saucepan and cook the garlic for 2 minutes. Add the chilli flakes and cook for a further 30 seconds. Stir the rice into the cooked garlic and chilli, along with the parsley, sweetcorn and seasoning.
SERVES 4

RICE & PEAS

30 ml (2 tbsp) vegetable oil
1 onion, thinly sliced
100 g (4 oz) creamed coconut, dissolved in
600 ml (1 pint) boiling water
600 ml (1 pint) vegetable stock
350 g (12 oz) long-grain rice
1 fresh red chilli, seeded and finely chopped
30 ml (2 tbsp) chopped fresh thyme
Salt and ground black pepper
150 g (5 oz) canned red kidney beans, rinsed
15 ml (1 tbsp) toasted desiccated coconut, to garnish
Thyme sprigs, to garnish

Heat the oil in a saucepan, add the onion and sauté for 5 minutes until golden. Add the coconut with its water, the stock, rice, chilli, thyme and seasoning to the pan. Cover the pan and simmer for 20 minutes, until the rice grains have swelled and most of the liquid has been absorbed.

Uncover the pan, stir the kidney beans into the rice and cook for a further 8-10 minutes, until the rice is tender and all the liquid has been absorbed. Garnish with toasted coconut and thyme and serve at once.
SERVES 6

TOP: Jasmine & Sesame Rice
BOTTOM: Rice & Peas

CHILLI BEANS

45 ml (3 tbsp) vegetable oil

1 medium onion, chopped

2 cloves garlic, crushed

10-15 ml (2-3 tsp) hot chilli powder

5 ml (1 tsp) cumin seeds

397-g (14-oz) can chopped tomatoes

150 ml (¼ pint) red wine

30 ml (2 tbsp) tomato purée

20 ml (4 tsp) molasses or treacle

432-g (15-oz) can red kidney beans, drained
and rinsed

432-g (15-oz) can black-eyed beans, drained
and rinsed

150 ml (¼ pint) water

Salt and ground black pepper

45 ml (3 tbsp) chopped fresh oregano

Heat the oil in a large saucepan, add the onion and garlic, and sauté for 3 minutes. Stir in the chilli and cumin and cook for a further minute.

Add the chopped tomatoes, wine, tomato purée and molasses, and simmer for 10 minutes. Add the two types of beans and the water. Season the chilli, cover and cook for a further 20 minutes. Stir in the oregano, taste and adjust seasoning, if necessary, and cook for a further 4-5 minutes. Serve the chilli beans hot as an accompaniment to barbecued potatoes, burgers or sausages. SERVES 6

SKEWERED NEW POTATOES

32 baby new potatoes, about 700 g (1½ lb) in
total weight

60 ml (4 tbsp) olive oil

Sea salt and ground black pepper

8 wooden skewers, soaked in cold water for
2 hours

HERB BUTTER

75 g (3 oz) butter, softened

30 ml (2 tbsp) chopped fresh herbs of your choice

Salt and ground black pepper

Scrub the potatoes and cook them in boiling, salted water for about 12 minutes or until tender.

Drain the potatoes and, while they are still warm, toss with the olive oil and plenty of salt and pepper. Thread four potatoes on to each skewer and set aside until required.

Mix the ingredients for the Herb Butter together. Place the butter in a sausage shape on a piece of greaseproof paper or cling film and roll up to produce a cylinder. Refrigerate the butter until it becomes firm enough to slice.

Cook the potatoes on a prepared barbecue for 12-15 minutes, turning them frequently. Serve hot with the Herb Butter. SERVES 8

RIGHT: Chilli Beans

GRILLED PEPPER & PASTA SALAD

175 g (6 oz) dried pasta shapes
4 halves sun-dried tomatoes in oil, drained and sliced
1 yellow pepper, grilled, skinned and sliced into strips
1 red pepper, grilled, skinned and sliced into strips
15 ml (1 tbsp) chopped fresh oregano
15 ml (1 tbsp) chopped fresh thyme

TAPENADE DRESSING

45 ml (3 tbsp) extra virgin olive oil
15 ml (1 tbsp) balsamic vinegar
1 clove garlic, crushed
5 ml (1 tsp) black olive tapenade
Salt and ground black pepper

Place the ingredients for the dressing in a screw-topped jar and shake well to combine. Taste and adjust seasoning, if necessary. Set aside until required.

Cook the pasta in boiling, salted water for 12-15 minutes until it is tender. Drain and transfer the pasta to a large bowl. Pour over the dressing and add the remaining ingredients. Toss to combine. If time permits, leave the salad to stand for 1 hour before serving to allow the flavours to develop. SERVES 4

CRISP GREEN SALAD

175 g (6 oz) mixed crisp lettuce leaves, such as Cos, iceberg and frisée, washed and torn into bite-sized pieces
2 sticks celery, sliced on the diagonal
1 small avocado, peeled, stoned and chopped
2 spring onions, sliced
75 g (3 oz) cucumber, chopped
50 g (2 oz) cashew nuts, toasted

CASHEW NUT DRESSING

75 g (3 oz) cashew nuts, toasted
90 ml (6 tbsp) sunflower oil
45 ml (3 tbsp) cider vinegar
2.5 ml (½ tsp) soft brown sugar
Salt and ground black pepper

Make the dressing. Place the cashew nuts in a food processor and grind coarsely. Add the oil, vinegar, sugar and seasoning and blend briefly to produce a thick, nutty dressing.

Place the prepared salad ingredients in a large bowl. Just before serving, pour over the dressing and toss gently to combine. Serve at once. SERVES 4-6

TOP: Crisp Green Salad
BOTTOM: Grilled Pepper & Pasta Salad

CORNMEAL MUFFINS

150 g (5 oz) coarse cornmeal
75 g (3 oz) self-raising flour
5 ml (1 tsp) baking powder
Pinch of salt
50 g (2 oz) butter
150 ml (¼ pint) milk
1 large egg, beaten
Butter for greasing

Preheat the oven to 200°C (400°F, Gas mark 6). Sift together the cornmeal, flour, baking powder and salt. Melt the butter in a small pan, and stir the milk and beaten egg into the melted butter.

Make a well in the centre of the sifted dry ingredients. Pour in the liquid mixture and beat together to produce a smooth batter.

Grease eight muffin tins and divide the mixture between the tins. Bake in the oven for 18-20 minutes until risen and golden. Allow the muffins to cool in the tins before removing them.   MAKES 8 MUFFINS

BASIL AND PARMESAN MUFFINS

Add 16 chopped green olives, 12 coarsely chopped basil leaves and 60 ml (4 tbsp) grated Parmesan cheese to the prepared muffin batter. Sprinkle 30 ml (2 tbsp) grated Parmesan over the muffins once they are in the tins, and bake as described in the main recipe.

HERB MUFFINS

Add 60 ml (4 tbsp) chopped fresh herbs of your choice to the prepared muffin batter, then bake as described in the main recipe.

CHEESE MUFFINS

Add 50 g (2 oz) grated Gruyère cheese to the prepared muffin batter. Spoon the mixture into tins and sprinkle with an additional 50 g (2 oz) grated Gruyère. Bake as described in the main recipe.

OLIVE, BASIL & PARMESAN CIABATTA

1 loaf ciabatta bread
100 g (4 oz) butter, softened
6 stuffed green olives, finely chopped
90 ml (6 tbsp) grated Parmesan cheese
10 large basil leaves, torn
Salt and ground black pepper

Cut slices in the ciabatta loaf, cutting almost through to the base. Mix the butter, olives, Parmesan, basil and salt and pepper together. Spread the flavoured butter liberally on the cut slices of the ciabatta. Wrap the loaf in foil and place it on one side of a prepared barbecue for 20-30 minutes, until the butter has melted and the bread is hot. Serve at once.   MAKES 1 LOAF

GARLIC & SUN-DRIED TOMATO CIABATTA

1 loaf ciabatta bread
100 g (4 oz) butter, softened
20 ml (4 tsp) sun-dried tomato paste
5 ml (1 tsp) fennel seeds
2 large cloves garlic, crushed
Salt and ground black pepper

Cut slices in the ciabatta loaf, as described in the recipe above. Mix the remaining ingredients together, then prepare and cook the bread as described above.
MAKES 1 LOAF

TOP: Cornmeal Muffins
BOTTOM: Garlic & Sun-dried Tomato Ciabatta

INDEX